Doris Miller
HERO OF PEARL HARBOR

Bill O'Neal

EAKIN PRESS Fort Worth, Texas
www.EakinPress.com

About the Cover

Doris Miller fought bravely against Japanese attackers at Pearl Harbor. The young African-American from Texas was one of the first sailors to earn the Navy Cross during World War II. He grew up on a farm near Waco and was a high school football star. Doris joined the U.S. Navy when he was nineteen and was aboard the battleship *West Virginia* on December 7, 1941. Later in the war he gave his life for his country. In the movie *Pearl Harbor* this heroic sailor was played by Academy Award winner Cuba Gooding, Jr.

Copyright © 2007
By Bill O'Neal
Published By Eakin Press
An Imprint of Wild Horse Media Group
P.O. Box 331779
Fort Worth, Texas 76163
1-817-344-7036
www.EakinPress.com
ALL RIGHTS RESERVED
1 2 3 4 5 6 7 8 9
ISBN-10: 1-934645-01-X
ISBN-13: 978-1-934645-01-7
Library of Congress Control Number 2007929968

*For my granddaughter
Kendall Brooke Henderson*

Pearl Harbor hero Doris Miller proudly wearing his Navy Cross. (Courtesy The Texas Collection, Baylor University, Waco)

THE SECRETARY OF THE NAVY
Washington, D.C. 20350

The President of the United States takes pleasure in presenting the NAVY CROSS to

DORIS MILLER
MESS ATTENDANT FIRST CLASS
UNITED STATES NAVY

For service as set forth in the following

CITATION:

For distinguished devotion to duty, extraordinary courage and disregard for his own personal safety during the attack on the Fleet in Pearl Harbor, Territory of Hawaii, by Japanese forces on December 7, 1941. While at the side of his Captain on the bridge, MILLER, despite enemy strafing and bombing and in the face of serious fire, assisted in moving his Captain who had been mortally wounded, to a place of greater safety, and later manned and operated a machine gun directed at enemy Japanese attacking aircraft until ordered to leave the bridge.

Aboard the USS West Virginia

Sunday Morning, December 7, 1941

Mess attendant Doris Miller began his duties early on Sunday morning, December 7, 1941. Miller was one of nearly 1,500 sailors who made up the crew of the USS *West Virginia*.

The *West Virginia* was a **battleship** stationed at Pearl Harbor, Hawaii. There was a large U.S. naval base at Pearl Harbor. Ninety-six ships of the U.S. Navy were in Pearl Harbor on Sunday.

There were eight battleships at Pearl Harbor. These great ships were **moored** alongside each other on "Battleship Row" near Ford Island.

A battleship was a floating city. There was a barber shop and a laundry and a hospital and a dentist's office. The ships had baseball teams and boxing matches.

All of the crew members on the *West Virginia* knew Doris Miller. They called him "Dorie." Dorie Miller was a big man, standing six-foot-three and weighing 225 pounds. Dorie was a fine athlete. As a boxer Dorie won the heavyweight championship on the *West Virginia*.

Dorie was twenty-two years old. He had joined the Navy when he was nineteen. Dorie was an African-American who had grown up on a farm near Waco, Texas.

On the *West Virginia* Dorie was a **Mess Attendant** Second Class. Every day he arose early. Dorie awakened officers who had to go on duty. He helped to serve meals and clean the tables in the officers' **wardroom**.

Dorie earned extra pay by taking dirty clothes from the officers to the ship's laundry. He was picking up laundry on Sunday morning, December 7.

A few minutes before eight o'clock a powerful explosion shook the USS *West Virginia*. Immediately the battleship's alarm sounded, and the sailors were ordered to man their battle stations.

Dorie Miller's battle station was to carry ammunition to some of the ship's guns. Dorie ran up ladders to reach the deck of the *West Virginia*.

Outside the sky was filled with Japanese planes. There were hundreds of torpedo planes and bombers and fighters. The *West Virginia* continued to be struck by torpedoes. Bombs exploded on and near the big ship. Machine gun bullets from Japanese planes hit the battleship.

In the confusion most of the ship's guns were not in action. Dorie Miller reached his battle station, ready to carry ammunition and help with the wounded.

"The **captain** has been wounded!"

This shout came from the bridge, the command post of the *West Virginia*. An officer ordered Dorie Miller to come and help.

With bullets flying all around him, the big sailor began climbing toward the bridge. Within the next few minutes Dorie Miller would become one of the first American heroes of World War II.

Waco, Texas
1919–1939

Doris Miller was born in a three-room farm house on October 12, 1919. He was the third of four sons of Mr. and Mrs. Connery Miller. His older brothers were named Selvia and Connery, Junior.

After having two little boys his mother, Henrietta, wanted a baby girl. The midwife who helped Henrietta Miller give birth was sure that the third baby would be a girl. Henrietta and the midwife liked the name "Doris."

The third baby turned out to be a boy. But Henrietta used the name Doris anyway. Although Connery did not like the name for his new son, his wife thought it was a pretty name.

A few years later Doris got a little brother. Connery and Henrietta named their fourth son Arthur.

The four Miller boys grew up on a farm near the communities of Willow Grove and Speegleville. The Miller home was in the country a few miles northwest of Waco.

Connery Miller was a **tenant farmer** on land owned by W. C. Frazier. Connery farmed Frazier's land and earned a share of the crops

Willow Grove community centered around its school and church. The little school now is used as a community center. The Willow Grove Baptist Church may be seen back of the old school. (Photo by the author)

he produced. As their family grew, Connery and Henrietta added a couple of rooms. Their house finally had five rooms.

The boys had to help with the farm chores. But the four Miller boys loved to hunt and fish in the country. They learned to swim in nearby creeks.

The boys hunted with their father's single-shot .22 rifle. With only one shot the hunter had to hit the rabbit or squirrel with the first bullet or the animal would run away. Doris became a good shot. And he liked to preserve the animals he killed. Taxidermy became his hobby. He carefully stuffed and sewed the carcasses of squirrels and rabbits and birds.

Along with farm chores, the Miller brothers helped with house work. Henrietta taught the boys to sew and to wash and iron their clothes. They learned to cook on the wood-burning stove in the kitchen. The boys cut and stacked wood for the stove.

Henrietta was a devoted Christian. She had met Connery at a church service. She read her Bible every day. On Sundays the family would ride to church in their farm wagon.

The Miller boys went to school at Willow Grove and at other rural schools near their farm. School started in September each year. But cotton was picked in September. So the Miller brothers and other farm boys had to start school late every year.

The Miller brothers loved to play baseball and football with other schoolboys. Doris was big and husky, and he played rough with other little boys. He threw a baseball left-handed.

Willow Grove and other small rural schools only taught seven grades. There were no high schools in the country near the Miller home. But a few miles away, in Waco, was A. J. Moore High School.

Schools in Texas and other southern states were segregated. White children went to all-white schools. Black children attended all-black schools with African-American teachers. A. J. Moore High School was the city of Waco's African-American high school.

When Doris Miller was a teenager in the 1930s he attended Moore High School. Moore High School was a three-story brick building.

Doris enjoyed high school dances and he played on the football team. He was one of the biggest boys on the Moore High School squad. Doris played fullback and his teammates called him "Raging Bull."

But money was scarce in the Miller household. During the 1930s Americans suffered through the Great Depression. Most Americans were poor during the Depression.

Doris Miller attended Moore High School in Waco. (Courtesy The Texas Collection, Baylor University, Waco)

Before his senior year in high school Doris dropped out to go to work. He took a job in a Waco cafe to earn money for his family. He tried to enlist in the Civilian Conservation Corps. The CCC enrolled young men whose parents were unemployed. The young men worked for $30 per month, and $25 of their pay was sent home to their parents. But Connery Miller was employed on the farm of W. C. Frazier. Doris was not eligible for the CCC.

Since Doris could not join the CCC he tried to enlist in the U.S. Army. But he was too young to enlist without his parents' permission. Henrietta Miller did not want her son to leave high school for the army. She refused to give her permission.

In September 1939 World War II began in Europe. Adolf Hitler, the **dictator** of Germany, attacked one European nation after another. The United States was not yet involved, but many Americans believed that the U.S. Army and Navy should be expanded. Among the first Americans to enlist after the war began was Doris Miller.

The ammunition ship Pyro. The USS Pyro was the first ship on which Dorie Miller served. (Courtesy National Archives)

The USS West Virginia. The battleship was nicknamed the "Wee Vee." (Courtesy National Archives)

U.S. Navy
1939–1941

When World War II started in September 1939, Doris Miller was nineteen, and in October he would turn twenty. He was old enough to enlist in the armed forces without his parents' permission.

This time Doris would try the U.S. Navy. He traveled to Dallas. On September 16, 1939, Doris Miller enlisted at the Navy Recruiting Station in Dallas.

Doris returned home for two weeks with his family before training began. Then he boarded a train in Waco for the long trip to the Naval Training School in Norfolk, Virginia. After several weeks of training Doris was given the rating of Mess Attendant Third Class.

Like schools in the South, the U.S. Navy practiced a form of segregation. African-Americans could only serve as cooks and mess attendants. They were not trained in gunnery or any other duties beside kitchen work.

Doris knew that he would be a mess attendant in the Navy. But his mother had taught him to cook. And he had been working in a café in Waco. He told his friends that joining the Navy "beats sitting around Waco working as a busboy, going nowhere."

Mess Attendant Doris Miller was assigned to the ammunition ship *Pyro*. On January 2, 1940, Doris was transferred to the *West Virginia*. After several months he was sent to another battleship, the USS *Nevada*, for temporary duty. In August 1940 he returned to the *West Virginia*. By December 1941 Doris was aboard the *West Virginia* in Pearl Harbor.

By that time World War II had been raging

in Europe for more than two years. Everyone focused on the European war. But on the other side of the world, Japan worked to expand its Pacific empire. Japanese leaders wanted growth, even if it meant attacking and conquering weaker countries. With everyone watching Europe, only the United States stood in the way of Japan's conquests in the Pacific.

In the Pacific the United States owned the Hawaiian Islands, the Philippine Islands, and several smaller islands. To protect these possessions there was a large army force in the Philippines and the Pacific **Fleet** at Pearl Harbor in Hawaii.

Japanese leaders decided that they should attack America's Pacific Fleet in Pearl Harbor. Americans would never expect such an attack. Some Americans thought the Japanese might attack the Philippines, much closer to Japan.

But the Japanese began planning a surprise attack against Pearl Harbor. If they could sink the U. S. Pacific Fleet there would be no one to stop them from conquering weak countries in the Pacific. Japanese military leaders assembled a

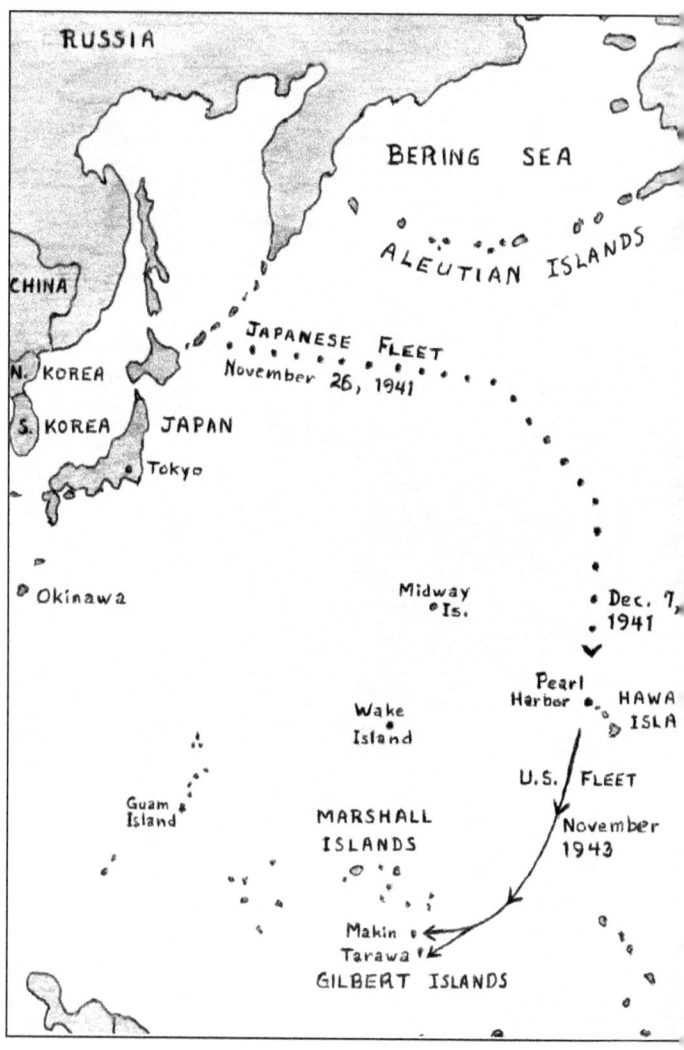

fleet of thirty-one ships. The biggest and most important of these ships were six **aircraft carriers**.

These aircraft carriers would launch 353 planes against American forces in Hawaii. The Japanese fleet would sail in secret from Japan toward Hawaii. When they were 275 miles north of Pearl Harbor, the aircraft carriers would launch their attack planes.

The attack would take place early on Sunday morning, December 7. The Japanese had learned that many American soldiers and sailors were given weekend passes. The Americans would spend Saturday night or all weekend having fun in the city of Honolulu. With many sailors and officers off-duty on Sunday mornings, ships were undermanned. On December 7 four of the eight battleship commanders were away from their ships.

The most important targets were three U.S. Navy aircraft carriers. But the Japanese did not know that all three of these carriers had sailed out of Pearl Harbor toward other assignments. With the carriers missing, the biggest targets in Pearl Harbor were the battleships.

All eight battleships in the Pacific Fleet were in Pearl Harbor on December 7. The *Pennsylvania* was in drydock undergoing repair work. The other seven battleships were moored along "Battleship Row" near Ford Island. The *California* and the *Nevada* were at opposite ends of Battleship Row. The *Arizona* was in front of the *Nevada*. The *Tennessee* and the *West Virginia* were moored beside each other. The *Oklahoma* and the *Maryland* also were side-by-side.

A little before eight o'clock on Sunday morning the Japanese planes arrived above Pearl Harbor. The fighter planes attacked the

American planes on the ground at nearby airfields. Japanese torpedo planes and bombers went after the battleships. One of the first Japanese torpedoes hit the USS *West Virginia*.

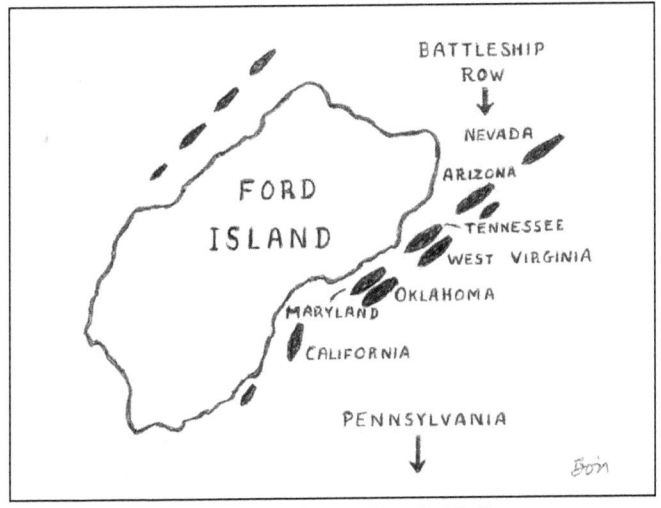

Ford Island, December 7, 1941.

Pearl Harbor
December 7, 1941

The commander of the USS *West Virginia* was Captain Mervyn Bennion. Captain Bennion was in charge of a ship that had been completed in 1923.

The *West Virginia* was more than 600 feet long with a beam (width) of nearly 100 feet. The battleship was heavily armored with steel plate. The eight big guns could fire their huge shells a distance of nearly twenty miles. There were many other guns, including anti-aircraft guns.

Captain Bennion had carefully trained his large crew. But the Japanese attack came without warning. Immediately the *West Virginia* was shaken by the powerful blast of a torpedo.

The alarm for **General Quarters** was sounded. Captain Bennion led his men in rushing to battle stations. The captain reached the bridge and began directing his ship's defense.

Torpedoes continued to slam into the *West Virginia*. A total of seven torpedoes struck the battleship. Holes were torn in the side of the *West Virginia*. Water began to flood the big ship. Two bombs from above exploded on the decks. Fires started and thick smoke swirled across the ship. Crew members were killed by the explosions and by machine gun bullets from the Japanese planes.

TORPEDO

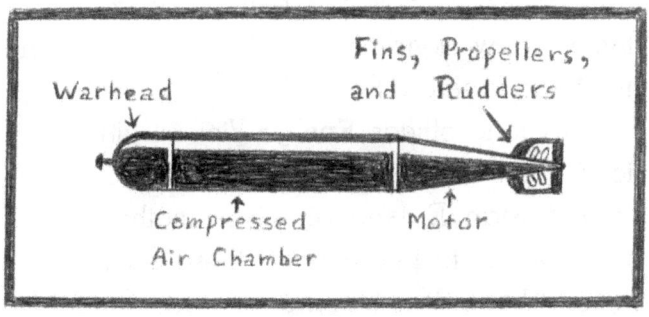

A torpedo is a self-propelled underwater projectile. Torpedoes are launched against ships by submarines, destroyers, and torpedo-bomber airplanes.

Bombs began to hit the *Tennessee*, moored beside the *West Virginia*. One explosion hurled a piece of metal at the bridge of the *West Virginia*. The metal hit Captain Bennion and ripped open his stomach. The captain fell but continued to give orders.

By this time Dorie Miller had climbed on deck to his battle station. **Lieutenant Commander** Dior Johnson ran past on his way to the bridge. Johnson ordered big Dorie to come with him and help.

On the bridge they found Captain Bennion, wounded and in pain. Johnson and Dorie carried the captain to a sheltered area. Captain Bennion asked how the battle was going. As flames grew near he urged the men around him to go to safety. Soon Captain Bennion died.

A young officer, **Ensign** Victor Delano, noticed two machine guns that were not being fired. Ensign Delano directed another officer and a sailor to begin firing these guns. Dorie Miller, who had no training on guns, was sent to pass ammunition.

Moments later Ensign Delano looked back

at the machine guns. Dorie Miller was not passing ammunition. He had taken over one of the guns. Dorie was shooting at the swarm of enemy planes. Ensign Delano saw that Dorie was smiling as he operated the machine gun. Dorie was quiet and almost never smiled. The only other time that Ensign Delano had seen him smile was when he had won the ship's heavyweight boxing championship.

Dorie Miller had seen other sailors operate these guns. But he had never had gunnery training. Later Dorie was asked how he had fired the gun.

"It wasn't hard," replied Dorie. "I just pulled the trigger and she worked fine. I had watched the others with these guns. I guess I fired her for about fifteen minutes. I think I got one of those planes. They were diving pretty close to us."

While Dorie was shooting at the Japanese planes his ship was sinking. Just behind the *West Virginia* the *Arizona* had exploded and sunk. Over 1,100 *Arizona* crew members were killed. In front of the *West Virginia* the *Oklahoma* **capsized**, trapping many sailors inside.

The USS West Virginia *is burning and sinking on December 7, 1941. The battleship was struck by seven Japanese torpedoes and two bombs. Doris Miller performed heroically on the bridge. The battleship* Tennessee *may be seen behind the* West Virginia. (Courtesy National Archives)

The *West Virginia* also was in danger of capsizing. The big ship was listing to one side. But alert crew members operated the necessary valves for counterflooding. The *West Virginia* settled upright in the shallow water.

The order to abandon ship was given. Many men stayed aboard to fight fires. Other sailors climbed onto the nearby *Tennessee* to help control damage on a sister ship.

When the enemy planes flew back toward their carriers they left behind burning ships and planes. Seven of the eight American battleships were sunk or badly damaged. Three smaller ships were reduced to junk. The Japanese had destroyed 188 American planes and damaged 150 more. Almost 2,400 Americans were killed, including Captain Bennion and 104 crew members of the *West Virginia*.

Americans exploded with anger when they learned of the "sneak attack" on Pearl Harbor. The next day, December 8, 1941, the United States declared war on Japan.

The American people wanted revenge for Pearl Harbor. Eventually Americans destroyed all thirty-one of the Japanese ships that had made up the Pearl Harbor attack fleet. America's Pacific Fleet was rebuilt. For example, the *West Virginia* was refloated and repaired. In 1944 the "Wee Vee," as the sailors called it, joined the war against Japan.

But in December 1941 such successes were far in the future. After the Pearl Harbor disaster American morale needed a boost. Americans needed heroes. Dorie Miller soon would be recognized as a hero of Pearl Harbor.

Hero of Pearl Harbor
1942–1943

News about Dorie Miller's heroism was slow to reach the public. Secretary of the Navy Frank Knox ordered a news blackout about details of the Pearl Harbor attack. For ten days there was no news from Pearl Harbor. Secretary Knox flew to Pearl Harbor to learn firsthand what had happened.

When news began to be released, Americans learned about men who had performed bravely during the attack. Secretary Knox mentioned a "seaman aboard a battleship" who "single-handedly manned a machine gun and blasted an attacking torpedo plane as it leveled against his ship." But Secretary Knox failed to mention the name of this courageous sailor—Dorie Miller.

"A Negro mess attendant who never had fired a gun manned a machine gun on the bridge until the ammunition was exhausted...." This news release came from an officer on another ship who had seen Dorie in action. But this officer did not know Dorie's name.

Rumors spread that this "Negro mess attendant" had shot down as many as four of the attacking planes. Twenty-nine Japanese planes had been shot down. Another seventy enemy planes were hit but managed to fly back to their aircraft carriers.

It is impossible to know how many planes Dorie might have hit. Hundreds of guns were firing from the ninety-six American ships in Pearl Harbor.

"I think I got one of those planes," said Dorie.

Several Japanese planes were shot down by American pilots who defended Pearl Harbor with their fighter planes. Six of these pilots were officially praised by the U.S. War Department. But still no one even knew the name of the heroic "Negro mess attendant" from the *West Virginia*.

The *Pittsburgh Courier*, a newspaper for African-Americans, demanded to know the name of "the colored messman." The NAACP (National Association for the Advancement of Colored People) also demanded to know the name.

The Navy Department finally responded to this pressure in March 1942, three months after Pearl Harbor. The Navy identified the *West Virginia* hero as Doris Miller of Waco, Texas. Secretary Knox sent a letter of commendation to Doris.

"We would like to know why it required so long to identify Mr. Miller," asked the *Pittsburgh Courier*, "and why to date he has received no reward for his heroism."

Other African-American newspapers also demanded a medal for Doris Miller. The NAACP added its influence. So did the National Negro Congress, the Southern Negro Youth Council, and many other African-American organizations.

At last Secretary Knox announced that Doris

Miller would be awarded the Navy Cross. The Navy Cross is the Navy's second highest award. Only the Congressional Medal of Honor—an award given by the U.S. Congress—is higher. Doris Miller would become the first African-American ever to receive the Navy Cross.

Doris Miller was presented the Navy Cross on May 27, 1942. On that date medals were presented to Miller and eight other honorees. Miller was the only African-American honoree.

The award ceremony was held on the USS *Enterprise*. The *Enterprise* was an aircraft carrier, one of the largest ships in the U.S. Navy. The *Enterprise* had a crew of more than 2,000 men.

The aircraft carrier Enterprise. *Dorie Miller was presented his Navy Cross on the flight deck of the USS* Enterprise. (Courtesy National Archives)

Most of these crew members stood at attention during the award ceremony.

The awards were presented by **Admiral** Chester W. Nimitz. Admiral Nimitz was Commander in Chief of the Pacific (CINCPAC). President Franklin D. Roosevelt promoted Admiral Nimitz soon after the disaster at Pearl Harbor. Admiral Nimitz was a Texan, like Doris Miller. The admiral's hometown was Fredericksburg, Texas.

Dorie Miller (center) being presented the Navy Cross. The ceremony was held on the USS Enterprise. (Courtesy National Archives)

Admiral Nimitz pinned the Navy Cross on the uniform of Doris Miller. The admiral congratulated Doris.

"This marks the first time ... that such high tribute has been made in the Pacific Fleet to a member of his race," announced Admiral Nimitz, "and I am sure that the future will see others similarly honored."

Admiral Chester Nimitz pins the Navy Cross on the uniform of Dorie Miller. Both men were from Texas. (Courtesy National Archives)

Doris was promoted to Cook, Third Class. His mother had taught him to cook when he was a little boy. He was assigned to the USS *Indianapolis*.

The *Indianapolis* was a **cruiser**. A cruiser is faster but not as large as a battleship. The guns on a cruiser are not as large or as powerful as those on a battleship. There were about 550 crew members on the *Indianapolis*. (The battleship *West Virginia* had almost 1,500 crew members.)

Dorie served on the *Indianapolis* for several months in 1942 and 1943. In 1942 Dorie was given a Christmas leave. He came home to Waco for the holiday. Citizens of Waco welcomed the hero of Pearl Harbor.

"The whole town was in chaos," said Dorie's

Dorie Miller served aboard the cruiser Indianapolis *for several months in 1942 and 1943.*

younger brother Arthur. "Everyone wanted to see the hero."

After spending Christmas with his family Dorie returned to duty. The Navy sent him on public appearances. The public appearances of military heroes were used to sell war bonds. American citizens and companies bought war bonds from the government. The government used these bonds to pay for ships, airplanes, tanks, ammunition, and other tools of war.

During World War II American industry produced 296,400 air-

Dorie Miller in his blue winter uniform while assigned to the USS Indianapolis. *Notice "Indianapolis" on his cap.* (Courtesy The Texas Collection, Baylor University, Waco)

Dorie Miller speaking on behalf of the war effort. Dorie is wearing his Navy Cross. (Courtesy National Archives)

planes and 86,330 tanks. Millions of uniforms and guns and bullets were produced. American shipyards built 6,500 ships for the Navy.

The shipyards built many new battleships and cruisers, submarines and aircraft carriers. There were hundreds of new **destroyers** and smaller ships. One new type of ship was the **escort carriers**.

Escort carriers were nicknamed "baby carriers." They were smaller than large carriers. Escort carriers could not carry as many planes. But since they were smaller than big carriers, escort carriers did not cost as much and could be built faster.

One of these escort carriers was the *Liscombe Bay*. In the spring of 1943 a crew was assembled for the new ship. On May 15, 1943, Dorie Miller was transferred to the *Liscombe Bay*. Soon the *Liscombe Bay* would be in battle in the Pacific.

USS Liscombe Bay
May 15–November 24, 1943

Fifty-five escort carriers of the *Casablanca* class were built for the U.S. Navy. The USS *Casablanca* was commissioned on July 8, 1943. During the next twelve months the other fifty-four ships were finished.

Fifty of these ships served with the Pacific Fleet. The other five served with the Atlantic Fleet. The USS *Liscombe Bay* was one of the first of the *Casablanca* class to be commissioned. The *Liscombe Bay* was commissioned in August 1943.

The *Liscombe Bay* and its crew sailed into the Pacific to fight the enemy. The flight deck was crowded with new planes being carried into the Pacific war.

The flight deck on the *Liscombe Bay* was nearly 500 feet long and 105 feet wide. (All fifty-five of the *Casablanca* class carriers were the same size.) Escort carriers were lightly armed. The *Liscombe Bay* had one cannon and twenty-eight anti-aircraft guns.

Dorie Miller was a cook now. He spent most of his time working in the galley (kitchen) of the *Liscombe Bay*.

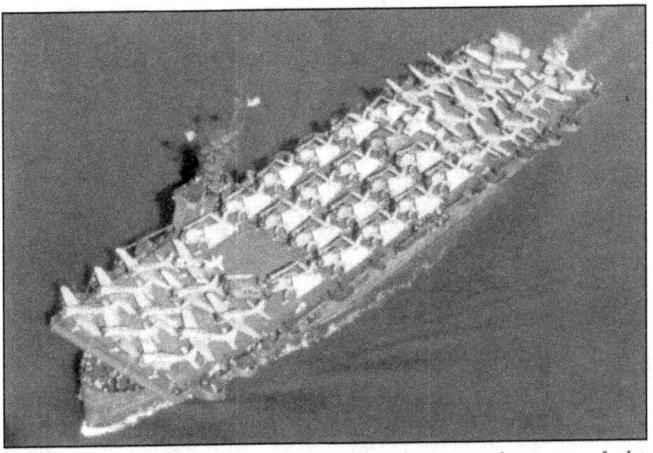

The USS Liscombe Bay, *loaded with new planes to fight against Japanese in the Pacific. The escort carrier was Dorie Miller's last ship.* (Courtesy National Archives)

In November 1943 the *Liscombe Bay* became part of an attack force. This force would include the Gilbert Islands.

After Pearl Harbor the Japanese had attacked and captured several U.S. islands in the Pacific. But in June 1942 U.S. forces began to defeat the Japanese in battle. Then U.S. forces started to fight their way toward Japan.

In September 1942 the Japanese Navy had captured the Gilbert Islands. But in November 1943 a large U.S. fleet sailed out of Pearl Harbor toward the Gilbert Islands. Americans wanted to capture Makin Island and Tarawa in the Gilberts. Americans planned to operate airfields from these islands. American planes would fly from these airfields to attack the next group of islands, the Marshall Islands.

The *Liscombe Bay* was part of the fleet that sailed out of Pearl Harbor in November 1943. When the fleet approached the Gilbert Islands the ships split into two groups. One **task force** attacked Tarawa. The other task force attacked Makin Island. The *Liscombe Bay* was part of the attack against Makin Island.

On November 13 planes from the *Liscombe Bay* and other carriers began bombing Makin Island. After a week of bombing, Makin Island was invaded by soldiers from the task force. The invasion was on November 20. The soldiers fought for four days. On Thanksgiving Day, November 24, the Americans took control of Makin Island.

During the battle planes took off and landed onto the *Liscombe Bay*. The ship's crew and pilots were busy for days. Dorie Miller and other cooks worked in the galley to keep the men fed.

Nine Japanese submarines were sent to fight the U.S. Navy in the Gilbert Islands. On November 24 submarine I-175 torpedoed the *Liscombe Bay*. The ship was hit at 6:15 in the morning, when Dorie was preparing breakfast for the crew.

The torpedo struck the carrier aft (rear). Suddenly there were fires and explosions. The *Liscombe Bay* sank rapidly. (A few months later the I-175 was sunk by American destroyers.)

The *Liscombe Bay* went down so fast that most of the crew members were trapped. About

200 men escaped. They were rescued from the water by other ships. But 644 men died on the *Liscombe Bay*.

Rear Admiral Henry M. Mullinex died. Captain I. D. Wiltse, commander of the *Liscombe Bay*, died. And the hero of Pearl Harbor, Dorie Miller, died.

The men who went down with the ship were declared missing by the Navy. The family of Dorie Miller hoped that somehow he had survived.

"At first," said Arthur Miller, the youngest brother, "we all hoped he would show up."

But he did not show up. One year after the *Liscombe Bay* sank, the missing sailors were officially declared dead.

The Miller family was grief-stricken by the death of Doris. But all three of his brothers joined the U.S. Army. And all three returned home safely after the war.

Honoring Doris Miller

Doris Miller was one of the first American heroes of World War II. But less than two years after Pearl Harbor he was killed in battle. During his wartime service Doris earned many awards from the Navy.

The Navy Cross
Asiatic-Pacific Campaign Service Medal
American Defense Service Medal
with Fleet Clasp
Purple Heart
World War II Medal
Good Conduct Medal

His medals were proudly displayed in the Miller home. The Miller family left the farm during the war. They moved to a house in Waco.

Mrs. Miller placed pictures of Doris beside his medals.

Mrs. Miller wanted another medal for Doris. She wanted Congress to give him the Medal of Honor. Other people also thought that the Medal

Medals earned by Doris Miller.

of Honor should be given for the heroism of Doris at Pearl Harbor.

Despite many requests a Medal of Honor was never awarded. But there were many other honors in his memory. In Waco a number of places have been named after Doris:

Doris Miller Elementary School
Doris Miller YMCA
Doris Miller Day Care Center
Doris Miller Memorial Park

The first memorial to Doris Miller was a stone marker placed at Moore High School in 1944.
(Courtesy The Texas Collection, Baylor University, Waco)

At the Waco Veterans Medical Center an eight-foot-tall granite marker stands in his honor.

This granite marker stands at the Veterans Administration Medical Center in Waco. The marker is eight feet tall. (Photo by the author)

Schools are named for Doris in Houston, Texas and Philadelphia, Pennsylvania. Doris Miller Auditorium stands in a park in Austin, Texas. Doris Miller VFW (Veterans of Foreign Wars) Post is in Los Angeles, California.

Doris Miller YMCA in Waco. The Doris Miller Day Care Center is in back. (Photo by the author)

Doris Miller Elementary School in Waco. (Photo by the author)

In 1970 the Miller Dining Hall was opened at Chase Field, the Naval Air Station in Beeville, Texas. The new dining hall was opened on June 2, 1970. The family of Doris Miller was invited to attend the ribbon-cutting ceremony.

Connery Miller had died in 1949 at the age of seventy-four. He was buried in Doris Miller Memorial Park. But Henrietta Miller was alive and well. Doris' mother attended the ceremony. So did his two brothers, Selvia and Arthur.

Doris Miller Memorial Park in Bellmead, a suburb of Waco. Doris's parents are buried here. (Photo by the author)

Marker to the memory of Doris Miller in the Doris Miller Memorial Park.

The next year Henrietta and Arthur attended another ceremony honoring Doris. The Doris Miller Bachelor Enlisted Quarters was dedicated at the Service School Command Naval Training Center in Great Lake, Illinois. The ceremony was held on December 7, 1971— the thirtieth anniversary of the attack on Pearl Harbor. Henrietta Miller was moved to tears when the heroism of her son was praised.

There was an even more important ceremony in 1973. The Navy awarded its highest honor to Doris Miller. A ship was named for the hero of Pearl Harbor.

The Destroyer Escort USS *Miller* was commissioned at the Norfolk Naval Ship Yard in Virginia. The ceremony was held on Saturday, June 30, 1973. The main speaker was Texas Congresswoman Barbara Jordan, a famous African-American.

Seated beside Congresswoman Jordan was Henrietta Miller. Doris Miller's mother now was seventy-eight. The Navy had flown Henrietta, her sister, and Arthur Miller to Norfolk. Also at the ceremony was a crowd of 750 people.

The highlight of the ceremony was the christening of the USS *Miller*. It is an old custom to christen a new ship by smashing a bottle of champagne against the hull. As honored guest, Henrietta Miller christened the ship named after her brave son. She swung the bottle of champagne against the steel hull. The bottle shattered. The crowd clapped and cheered.

The USS *Miller* now was part of the Navy. A fast and powerful warship carried the name of Doris Miller back to sea.

Henrietta Miller died in 1982 while in her eighties. She was buried beside her husband in Doris Miller Memorial Park.

Doris Miller's heroism at Pearl Harbor has been preserved on film. In 1970 *Tora! Tora! Tora!* was shown at movie theaters around the world. *Tora! Tora! Tora!* told the story of the attack on Pearl Harbor. One of the battle scenes showed Doris Miller firing a machine gun at enemy planes. Doris Miller was played by an African-American actor named Elven Havard. But the scene lasted only a few seconds.

There was a much fuller movie version of

Dorie Miller in *Pearl Harbor*. This 2001 film include Cuba Gooding, Jr., as Dorie Miller. Gooding was a popular actor. He won an Academy Award for acting in the 1996 movie, *Jerry Maguire*.

Gooding's first scene in Pearl Harbor was a boxing match. Gooding, as Dorie Miller, won the match and the heavyweight championship of the *West Virginia*. In his biggest scene, Dorie Miller pulls his wounded captain to a safer place. He speaks words of comfort to his dying captain. Then he begins firing a big machine gun. Dorie shoots down one of the Japanese planes.

There are other scenes showing Cuba Gooding as Dorie Miller. The movie *Pearl Harbor* offers a fine tribute to the brave sailor from Texas.

In 2004 a television program honored Doris Miller. *Waco's Hometown Hero, Doris Miller* was presented by WCCC-10, the Waco City Cable Channel. This half-hour program celebrates the memory of Doris. The East Waco Public Library has copies of *Waco's Hometown Hero* on video discs.

There have been many other tributes and honors for Dorie Miller. Dorie was a hero at Pearl Harbor. Then he lost his life in the service of his country. Dorie earned every honor he was given.

"Miller gave up his life in defense of freedom," said Congresswoman Barbara Jordan. "Destroyer escort *Miller* has been brought to life to pursue that same defense. It is a fitting tribute to the ultimate sacrifice of this man."

The USS Miller *was named after the hero of Pearl Harbor. Naming a ship after a sailor is the Navy's highest honor. The* Miller *was commissioned in 1973 and christened by Doris Miller's mother.*

Insignia designed for the USS Miller.

Words to Know

capsize—a sinking ship sometimes will turn upside down, or capsize.

commission—a document issued by the President appointing a man or woman a commissioned officer in the U.S. Armed Forces. In the U.S. Navy the officer with the lowest rank is an **ensign**. Next is a **lieutenant junior grade**, **lieutenant**, **lieutenant commander**, **commander**, **captain**, **rear admiral**, **vice admiral**, and **admiral**.

dictator—a ruler of a country with absolute power and authority.

fleet—a large group of warships. A **task force** is a smaller group of warships.

general quarters—an order for sailors to run to their battle stations on a ship.

mess attendant—a group of sailors who eat together are part of the mess. A mess attendant helps to serve and clean up after meals.

moor—in a harbor a ship is moored, or held in place, by ropes and cables or anchors.

tenant farmer—a tenant farmer lives on a farm and works the land, but does not own the land.

wardroom—the dining and living room for officers on a ship.

Ships of the U.S. Navy

- **Aircraft Carriers** were named after famous ships, battles, or men.

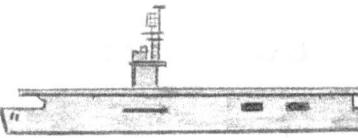

- **Escort Carriers** were nicknamed "Baby Carriers" and "Jeep Carriers."

- Doris Miller was killed while serving on the escort carrier *Liscombe Bay*.

- **Battleships** were named after states.

- Doris Miller was on the *West Virginia* during the Pearl Harbor attack.

- **Cruisers** were named after cities.

- Doris Miller served on the *Indianapolis*.

- **Destroyers** were named after Navy heroes.

- The destroyer *Miller* was named after Doris Miller.
- U.S. destroyers sank the Japanese submarine which sank the *Liscombe Bay*.

"USS" is short for "United States Ship," which means that a ship such as the USS *West Virginia* is part of the U.S. Navy.

Want to know more?

At Pearl Harbor in Hawaii you may visit the USS *Arizona* Memorial and the USS *Missouri*. In Waco, Texas, you may visit many memorials to Doris Miller, as described in the last chapter in this book.

The following Websites offer fascinating information about Pearl Harbor, Doris Miller, and the ships on which he served:

www.eyewitnesstohistory.com/pearl.htm
www.nps.gov/usar
www.DorisMiller.com
www.usswestvirginia.org

About the Author

Bill O'Neal was named "Best Living Nonfiction Writer for 2007" by *True West* magazine. Bill has written thirty books about western history, western movies, and baseball. He has appeared on television shows about history on The Learning Channel, A & E, The History Channel, TBS, and TNN. Bill taught history for thirty-three years at Panola College in Carthage, Texas. He won many teaching awards, including a Piper Professorship.

www.ingramcontent.com/pod-product-compliance
Lightning Source LLC
Chambersburg PA
CBHW071316060426
42444CB00036B/3069